A tree for spring

Story by Beverley Randell

Illustrated by Naomi Lewis

One day, Ben came to school
with some yellow flowers.

The teacher said,
"Thank you, Ben.
They are beautiful.
I love spring flowers."

4

"I love spring flowers, too,"
said Rose.
"Look at that tree, by the road.
It has little pink flowers on it."

"Yes," said the teacher.
"Spring is coming."

Then the teacher
showed the children
a little tree in a flower pot.

She said,
"Can you help me
make this little tree
look beautiful for the spring?"

The children looked
at the little gray tree in the pot.

"That's not a very good tree,
is it?" said Matt.

"It's too old," said Ben.

But Rose said,
"We can make some pink flowers.
They will make the little tree
look beautiful."

The children made
lots of little pink flowers.

"Let's make
   some green leaves for the tree,"
said Matt.

"Yes," said Rose.
"Trees get new green leaves
   in the spring."

14

"I have made a bird,"
said Ben.

"It's flying up
to the top of the tree," said Matt.

"I love your blue bird, Ben,"
said the teacher.

"Oh," said Matt.
"The tree looks beautiful, now."